Changes
Dressing Up
by Liz Gogerly

HODDER
Wayland

an imprint of Hodder Children's Books

Project manager: Liz Gogerly
Designer: Peta Morey
Picture Research: Shelley Noronha at Glass Onion Pictures
Consultant: Norah Granger

Published in 2002 by Hodder Wayland, an imprint of
Hodder Children's Books

British Library Cataloguing in Publication Data
Gogerly, Liz
Dressing up. - (Changes ; 4)
1. Clothing and dress - Great Britain - History - 19th century - Juvenile literature
2. Clothing and dress - Great Britain - History - 20th century - Juvenile literature
3. Costume - Great Britain - History - 19th century - Juvenile literature
4. Costume - Great Britain - History - 20th century - Juvenile literature
I.Title
391'.00941'09034

ISBN 0 7502 3965 4

Printed and bound in
Italy by G. Canale & Co

Hodder Children's Books
A division of Hodder Headline Limited
338 Euston Road, London NW1 3BH

PICTURE ACKNOWLEDGEMENTS:
The publisher would like to thank the following for allowing their
pictures to be used in this publication:
AKG 7 (top); Camera Press 11 (bottom); Corbis 5 (bottom), 13 (bottom),
14 (bottom); Mary Evans 5 (top), 8 (top), 14 (top), 16 (top);
Eye Ubiquitous/ James Davis Travel Photography 19 (bottom);
Angela Hampton 4 (bottom), 12 (bottom); Hodder Wayland Picture Library
10 (top); Hulton Getty 4 (top), 6 (top), 15 (top), 17 (top); Billy Love (title page),
9 (top); PhotoDisc (main cover); Photofusion 6 (bottom); Pictorial Press 9 (bottom), 15 (bottom); Popperfoto 7 (bottom); Topham Picturepoint (cover inset),
13 (top), 17 (bottom), 18 (top), 19 (top); Zul Mukhida 8 (bottom), 10 (bottom),
16 (bottom), 18 (bottom).

Contents

Dresses and Skirts

In **Victorian** times women and girls often wore long dresses or skirts. People thought bodies should be covered as much as possible. **Fashions** have changed a lot since then. These little girls are wearing short cotton dresses. The **material** is light and cool.

This **Victorian** girl is wearing a dress that covers her knees. When she was older she would have worn a longer dress. She is wearing a **corset** underneath. It makes her waist look tiny.

In the 1920s **fashionable** women and girls wore shorter skirts and dresses. By then most women did not wear **corsets**. Their bodies looked straight rather than curvy.

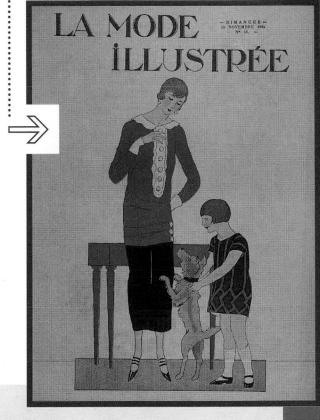

By the 1960s women could choose from many styles of dress and skirt. The woman on the right is wearing a **sari**. **Saris** are often made from cotton or **silk** so they feel cool.

Trousers and Shorts

This boy is wearing **combat trousers**. They look good and are **fashionable**. They are made from cotton so they feel soft. In the past males wore trousers or shorts made from thick **material** like wool. These were warm but they were not comfortable.

This **Victorian** boy is wearing breeches or short trousers. They match his jacket and **waistcoat**. His clothes look **formal** to us but boys often wore clothes like these every day.

For many years jeans were worn by workmen. These workmen from the 1930s are wearing jeans because they are strong and last a long time. Jeans became **fashionable** in the 1950s.

These boys from the 1960s are wearing shorts to school. Most boys wore shorts until they were about eleven. They felt grown up when they were allowed to wear long trousers.

What is on Top?

Most of us have **sweatshirts**, blouses, shirts, T-shirts, jumpers or jackets to wear. They come in lots of styles and colours. They are made from soft **materials**. They keep us cool in the summer or warm in the winter. In the past, children had far fewer choices.

Victorian and **Edwardian** children often wore **formal** clothes. Blouses and shirts were usually worn under stiff jackets. Try to imagine how uncomfortable these **Victorian** children would have felt on a hot day.

By the 1930s people liked to wear more **casual** tops. Two of these boys are wearing knitted jumpers. These felt soft and comfortable. Do you think they were warm too?

→

←

In the 1950s some people started to wear T-shirts. Until then mainly workmen had worn T-shirts. Many parents did not like their children to wear them because they looked too **casual**.

Underwear

The **Victorians** wore more underwear than we do today. Women wore **petticoats** and **bloomers**. Men wore **long johns** and vests. As **fashions** in clothes have changed, so have the clothes we wear underneath. New kinds of **material**, such as **Lycra**, mean that underwear is more comfortable too.

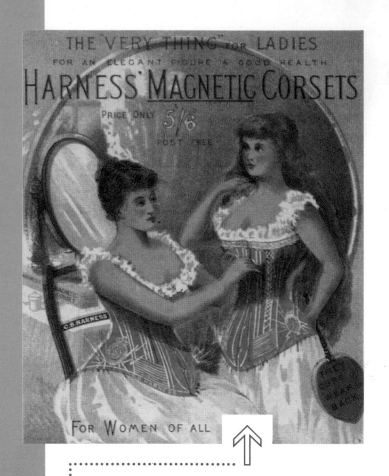

As well as layers of **petticoats Victorian** women and girls often wore **corsets**. These were pulled so tight that it was sometimes difficult to breathe properly.

These men from 1915 are wearing **long johns** and vests with long sleeves. They look a bit like pyjamas people wear now. In the past, people needed warm underwear because there was no **central heating**.

This is the pop star Madonna in the 1990s. By this time people were wearing their underwear as clothes. What do you think the **Victorians** would have thought about this **fashion**?

Hats Off!

In the past, nearly everybody had a hat. The **Victorians** expected people to wear their hats outdoors and to work. They thought it was rude if a man did not tip his hat to a woman. Today there are no rules about wearing hats. There are many kinds of hat too. **Baseball caps** and floppy sun hats are just two types.

This **Edwardian** girl is wearing a beautiful hat. It has a large **brim** and flowers made from **silk**. Girls often bought ribbons or flowers to make an old hat look pretty.

These children from the 1930s are wearing rain-hats. The hats have **brims** to keep the rain off their faces. The **brims** pull down over their ears to keep them warm.

These little boys from the 1950s are Sikhs. They are wearing **turbans** because it is part of their religion. How many children at your school wear **turbans** like these?

Neat Feet

These days we have lots of different kinds of shoe to choose from. We wear trainers for sport but we like to wear them every day too. We have **sandals** for the summer and boots for winter. In the past some children only had one pair of boots. They wore them until they fell apart.

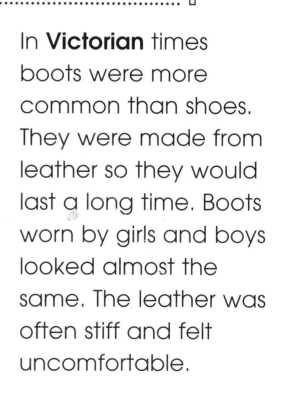

In **Victorian** times boots were more common than shoes. They were made from leather so they would last a long time. Boots worn by girls and boys looked almost the same. The leather was often stiff and felt uncomfortable.

Poorer families could not afford leather boots. Even in the 1920s some people wore wooden **clogs** because they were cheap. These lasted a long time but they were not very comfortable.

New **fashions** for shoes have come and gone over the years. Shoes and boots with **platform heels** were **fashionable** in the 1970s. They looked good but do you think they hurt people's feet?

Bits and Pieces

People have always enjoyed adding something extra to their clothes. Perhaps it is something they need like an umbrella or a watch. Or maybe it is something that looks good like a badge or a scarf. We do not always need these bits and pieces but they make dressing up more fun.

This **Victorian** girl is waving a fan to cool herself down. Fans were usually made from **silk** or paper. Sometimes they were hand-painted with beautiful designs.

In the past males usually wore **braces** to hold their trousers up. Belts were mainly used in sport. Then, in the 1920s, belts became more **fashionable** for every day. These boys are wearing both!

During the **Second World War** there was not enough **silk** to make **stockings**. Some women painted their legs with make-up or **gravy browning**. Do you think they look like real **stockings**?

What a Shock!

The **Victorians** were shocked if a woman showed her ankles. Now women can wear short skirts anywhere. In the past, men would not have worn skirts but they can now. Today, people can choose any **fashion** they like. Nothing seems to shock us any more!

This photograph was taken during the **First World War**. The women are wearing trousers, also called knickerbockers. This was shocking then but trousers were better for working in than long skirts.

Mini-skirts became **fashionable** in the 1960s. This photograph was taken at an important horse-race meeting called Royal Ascot in 1968. It was a surprise to see women dressed like this on that day.

People usually try to look their best when they dress up. In the 1970s the **punk** fashion was shocking because it looked so scruffy. Clothes often looked old and torn. Do you like this **fashion**?

Notes for Parents and Teachers

Changes and the National Curriculum

The books in this series have been chosen so that children can learn more about the way of life of people in the past. Titles such as *A Bite to Eat, Beside the Sea, Dressing Up, Home Sweet Home, School Days* and *Toys and Games* present children with subjects they already know about from their own experiences of life. As such these books may be enjoyed at home or in school, as they satisfy a number of requirements for the History Programme of Study at Key Stage 1.

These books combine categories from 'Knowledge, skills and understanding' and 'Breadth of study' as required by the National Curriculum. In each spread, the photographs are presented in chronological order. The first photograph is a modern picture that the child should recognize. The following pictures are all historical. Where possible, a wide variety of pictures, including paintings, posters, artefacts and advertisements, have been selected. In this way children can see the different ways in which the past is represented. A lively selection of pictures also helps to develop the children's skills of observation. In turn, this will encourage them to ask questions and discuss their own ideas.

The text is informative and raises questions for the children to talk about in class or at home. It is supported by further information about the historical photographs (see right). Once the children are familiar with the photographs you could ask them to guess when the pictures were taken – if it isn't mentioned in the text. By looking at clues such as clothes, hairstyles, style of buildings and vehicles they might be able to make reasonable guesses. There are further questions to ask your child or class on the right.

About the Photos

Dresses and Skirts
Pages 4–5

A girl posing on a swing in 1879.
Questions to ask:
- Do you think it would be easy to play sport in this dress?
- Do her boots look comfortable?

A mother and child on the cover of *La Mode Illustrée* in 1924.
Questions to ask:
- This woman's skirt might have been hard to walk in, can you think why?
- Do people dress like this today?

Indian royalty at a race-meeting, *circa* 1960.
Question to ask:
- What is the woman on the left holding in her hands?

Trousers and Shorts
Pages 6–7

A Victorian boy, date unknown.
Questions to ask:
- What is the boy wearing under his waistcoat?
- How do his shoes do up?

Workmen on the Rockefeller Center, New York, in 1932.
Questions to ask:
- Do you think these men's clothes look modern?
- How do your jeans look different?

Boys on their way home from primary school in 1961.
Questions to ask:
- Do boys of this age wear shorts to school now?
- How different is your school uniform from theirs?

What is on Top?
Pages 8–9

A fashion plate in *Journal des Demoiselles* in 1880.
Questions to ask:
- What material do you think these clothes were made from?
- Are these clothes similar to any of your clothes?

Children around a swing in 1931.
Question to ask:
- Can you think of another name for the jumper the boy at the front is wearing?

A photo of James Dean, 1950s.
Question to ask:
- Do you think this man would look fashionable today?

Underwear
Pages 10–11

A Victorian advertisement for magnetic corsets.
Questions to ask:
- Why do you think corsets can be bad for women's health?
- Are corsets still worn today?

Men posing in their long johns in 1915.
Question to ask:
- What material do you think these long johns were made from?

Madonna photographed at the Cannes Film Festival in 1998.
Questions to ask:
- Do you think that Madonna looks shocking in these clothes?
- What do older people in your family think about Madonna's clothes?

Hats Off!
Pages 12–13

Miss Campbell Beresford in April 1902.
Question to ask:
- When do women or girls wear hats like this now?

Children playing in Hyde Park in 1932.
Questions to ask:
- What else are the children wearing to keep warm?
- Do you think their coats are waterproof?

Indian children in London in 1952.
Questions to ask:
- Do you know how a turban is made?

Neat Feet
Pages 14–15

A selection of Victorian shoes and boots for men and women from *La Moniteur de la Cordonnerie*, 1880.
Questions to ask:
- Can you describe the different ways of doing up these shoes and boots?
- Can you tell which shoes are for women and which shoes are for men?

Women and children wearing clogs near Wigan, during the coal strike of 1921.
Questions to ask:
- How can you tell these children are poor?
- Describe the different clothes the children are wearing.

Dave Lee of Slade in his silver platform boots in the 1970s.
Question to ask:
- Why do you think platform heels are bad for your feet?

Bits and Pieces
Pages 16–17

A greeting card from 1890 showing a girl with a fan.
Questions to ask:
- What is painted on this fan?
- Do people ever use fans now?

Boys in belts and braces. Taken between the First and Second World Wars.
Questions to ask:
- Does anyone you know wear braces?
- What materials do you think belts can be made from?

Women in Croydon having their legs painted during the Second World War.
Question to ask:
- Do people do a similar kind of thing today?

What a Shock!
Pages 18–19

Women working at a salvage depot in 1918.
Questions to ask:
- What is holding the women's trousers up?
- What material do you think their trousers are made from?

Women in mini-skirts at Royal Ascot in 1968.
Questions to ask:
- Do you think these women's dresses look too short?
- Do you know what the men's hats are called?

Three young punk men together in London, *circa* 1980.
Questions to ask:
- Do you see people dressed like this where you live?
- Do you think their hairstyles are shocking?

Glossary

baseball cap A soft round hat worn by people who play the game baseball. It is now fashionable for anyone to wear.

bloomers Loose-fitting knickers that nearly reach the knees.

braces Two straps worn over the shoulders to hold up trousers.

brim The part that sticks out around the bottom of a hat.

casual Something relaxed. Casual clothes are usually worn when we are not working or going to an important occasion. Jeans and T-shirts are casual clothes.

central heating A system that heats water or air. The heated air or water is then carried around a building through pipes and radiators to heat up the whole place.

clogs Heavy shoes made from wood.

combat trousers Fashionable trousers which are like those worn by soldiers.

corset A tight-fitting piece of underwear that laces up at the back. The laces can be pulled tightly to make a person's waist look small.

Edwardian Used to describe anything or anybody from the time of King Edward VII (1901–1910).

fashion/ fashionable A style of dressing, or way of doing things that becomes popular at a certain time.

First World War The world war that started in 1914 and ended in 1918.

formal Formal clothes are usually worn for important occasions such as weddings or for certain jobs. A school uniform looks formal.

gravy browning A powder cooks add to their gravy to make it taste good and go dark brown.

long johns Tight-fitting cotton or wool trousers worn under everyday trousers.

Lycra A kind of material that feels soft and stretchy but lasts a long time.

material The cloth or fabric from which clothes are made. Wool, cotton, silk, nylon and Lycra are all materials.

petticoat A piece of underwear that looks like a dress. It is usually made from cotton or silk and is worn under a dress.

platform heels Very high, thick heels.

punk A style of music and dress that was popular in the 1970s.

sandals Light, open shoes that usually have straps that go over the feet.

sari A long piece of material that is wrapped around the body to make a dress. Saris are mainly worn by Indian, Pakistani or Bangladeshi women.

Second World War The world war that started in 1939 and ended in 1945.

silk A soft, light material that can be expensive to buy.

stockings Used to cover the legs. They fit tightly like socks but come up to the middle of the thigh and are often see-through.

sweatshirt A casual top with long sleeves and no collar. Usually made from a soft, warm material.

turban A long cloth wound around the head to cover the hair. Muslims, Hindus and Sikhs sometimes wear turbans.

Victorian Used to describe anything or anyone from the time when Queen Victoria ruled Britain (1837–1901).

waistcoat A short jacket with no sleeves. Usually worn under the jacket of a suit.

Further Information

Books to Read
Non-fiction
Looking Back: Clothes and Fashion by Joanne Jessop (Wayland, 1991)
Then and Now: Clothes and Fashion by A. Smith (Usborne Publishing, 1999)
20th Century Fashion: 1900–1920 by Sue Mee (Heinemann, 1999)

Fiction
Maisy's Favourite Clothes by Lucy Collins (Walker Books, 2001)
The Emperor's New Clothes by Hans Christian Andersen (Walker Books, 2000)
The Man who Wore all his Clothes by Allan Ahlberg and Katharine McEwan (Walker Books, 2001)

Sources
The Encyclopaedia of Fashion by Georgina O'Hara (Thames and Hudson, 1986)
Cover Up: A Curious History of Clothes by Richard Tames (Macdonald Young Books, 1995)

Websites
http://www.factmonster.com/ipka/ A0767725.html
This site has information and photographs about all kinds of clothes.

Website for Teachers
http://www.teachingideas.co.uk/ history/clothes.html
This site suggests an activity that requires the children to find out information about clothing of the past, so that they can make costumes for two models.

Museums to Visit
Childhood and Costume Museum
Newmarket Building, Postern Gate,
Bridgnorth WV16 4AA
Tel: 01746 764 636

Gallery of English Costume
Platt Hall, Rusholme, Manchester
M14 5LL
Tel: 0161 224 5217

Museum of Costume
Bennet Street, Bath BA1 2QH
Tel: 01225 477 789

Shambellie House Museum of Costume
New Abbey, Dumfriesshire
Tel: 01387 850 375

Victoria and Albert Museum
National Museum of Art and Design
Cromwell Road, South Kensington
London SW7 2RL
Tel: 020 7942 2000

Index